NATIONAL
GEOGRAPHIC

D0100743

The Story of Ice Cream

Ellen Marcus

Contents

Introduction

Do you love ice cream? If you do, you're not alone.
Ice cream is a part of everyday life for many people.
How did ice cream become a part of everyday life?
Let's trace the story of ice cream to find out.

Who Invented Ice Cream?

Some people think the leader of Rome, Emperor Nero, invented ice cream. Nero lived nearly 2,000 years ago. His cooks mixed snow with fruit, honey, or other **ingredients**. No one knows for sure whether or not this was the first ice cream.

We do know that about 350 years ago people in Europe ate a dessert made from flavored ice. Cooks added cream to the flavored ice to make a creamy treat. Only wealthy people enjoyed this dessert because ice was expensive to buy.

Emperor Nero loved food. He gave many parties with special treats for his guests.

Ice Cream in America

Americans first ate ice cream about 250 years ago. The **recipe** for ice cream was brought to America by people from Europe. People moving to America brought the recipe with them.

The recipe for making ice cream was easy to follow. Cooks put a bowl of cream, eggs, and sugar inside a bucket of ice. One cook stirred the cream mixture. Another cook shook the ice.

It took hours of stirring and shaking for the mixture to become ice cream. Because ice cream took so long to make, only a few people got to eat it. Ice cream was an expensive treat made in small amounts for wealthy people.

It took two cooks working together to make ice cream.

In 1843, Nancy Johnson invented an ice-cream maker called a **churn**. The ice-cream churn had a crank for stirring the ingredients. Its sides were packed with ice. Ice cream froze smoothly when it was made in a churn.

Johnson's churn made it easier and faster to make ice cream. However, it was still hard work to make lots of ice cream. In 1851, Jacob Fussell changed all that.

It takes about 50 licks to eat an ice-cream cone with one scoop.

In 1940, ice-cream churns like the one Nancy Johnson invented were still being used.

Ice Cream for Everyone

Jacob Fussell sold milk and cream in Baltimore. One day, in 1851, he had a large amount of cream left over. Instead of letting the cream go bad, he made it into ice cream. He sold the ice cream cheaply and many people bought it. Jacob decided to open an ice-cream **factory**.

By 1856, Fussell had opened factories in Boston and Washington, D.C. Making ice cream in factories made it less expensive. Now, many people could afford to buy ice cream. It became a popular treat.

July is National Ice Cream Month in the United States.

Jacob Fussell's partner, J.M. Horton, opened his own ice-cream factory in New York.

Sodas, Sundaes, and Cones

Soon, Americans began eating ice cream in new ways. In the 1870s, ice-cream sodas became popular. No one knows for sure who first added ice cream and sweet syrup to **soda**, or "bubbly water." But it tasted great!

Young people drank ice-cream sodas at soda shops in the 1950s.

During the 1880s, it was considered wrong to sell soda water on Sundays. So, stores started serving ice cream in a dish with syrup on top. The new "ice-cream Sunday" became popular. The name was changed to "sundae" because people began eating this treat every day, not just on Sunday.

The biggest ice-cream sundae ever made weighed 24 tons. It was made in Canada.

People started eating ice cream in a cone in the early 1900s. Many people believe the cone first appeared at the World's Fair in St. Louis, Missouri, in 1904. A **vendor** who was selling ice cream ran out of dishes. The vendor next to him was selling thin, waffle-shaped cakes. The waffle seller shaped his cakes into cones to hold the ice cream. No dishes needed!

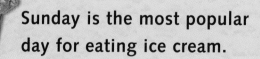

Sunday is the most popular day for eating ice cream.

We Love Ice Cream!

The story of ice cream is never ending. There are hundreds of flavors available today. Some flavors are quite strange, like ketchup, pickle, and even tuna. But the most popular flavor is good old vanilla. Yum! What's your favorite flavor?

Glossary

churn   a machine that shakes and mixes whatever is put inside it

factory   a building where products are made or put together

ingredient   one of several items combined to make food

recipe   a list of ingredients and instructions for how to make food

soda   water that has gas added to make bubbles

vendor   a person who sells something